READING POWER

Writing in the Ancient World

WRITING IN ANCIENT PHOENICIA

JIL FINE

The Rosen Publishing Group's
PowerKids Press™
New York

Published in 2003 by The Rosen Publishing Group, Inc.
29 East 21st Street, New York, NY 10010

First Edition

Book Design: Michael DeLisio and Sam Jordan

Photo Credits: Cover, Erich Lessing/Art Resource, NY; pp. 4, 14–15, 16–17 © North Wind Picture Archives; pp. 5, 8, 14, 18, 19 (maps and symbols) Michael DeLisio; p. 6 (left) Vanni Archive/Corbis; p. 6 (top right) © Corbis; pp. 6 (bottom right), 10 (bottom left) © David Lees/Corbis; p. 7 © Diego Lezama Orezzolli/Corbis; p. 8 Giraudon/Art Resource, NY; p. 9 © Paul Almasy/Corbis; p. 10 (top left) © Werner Forman/Corbis; p.10 (right) © National Geographic Image Collection; p. 11 Réunion des Musées Nationaux/Art Resource, NY; pp. 12–13 © Gianni Dagli Orti/ Corbis; p. 13 (inset) Wolfgang Kaehler/Corbis; p. 18 © Historical Picture Archive/Corbis; pp. 20–21 © National Gallery Collection, by kind permission of the Trustees of the National Gallery, London/Corbis

Library of Congress Cataloging-in-Publication Data

Fine, Jil.
Writing in ancient Phoenicia / Jil Fine.
    p. cm. — (Writing in the ancient world)
Summary: Explores how ancient Phoenicians adapted Mesopotamians' cuneiform into their own written language around 1500 B.C. then, through their trade with other nations, spread the alphabet to parts of Asia, Africa, and Europe.
ISBN 0-8239-6507-4
1. Phoenician language—Alphabet—Juvenile literature. 2. Alphabet—History—Juvenile literature. [1. Phoenician language—Alphabet. 2. Alphabet—History. 3. Writing—History. 4. Phoenicians.] I. Title. II. Series.
PJ4173 .F56 2003
492'.6—dc21

                                    2002000316

Contents

ANCIENT PHOENICIANS

Ancient Phoenicians lived near the east end of the Mediterranean Sea. They came to this area around 3000 B.C. Phoenicians were very good sailors. They were also traders who sailed from place to place, staying mostly along the seacoast.

CHECK IT OUT

▶ The Phoenicians were well-known in the ancient world for their purple dye. The dye came from a special snail. The word *phoenicia* is thought to have come from *phoinix*, which means "red purple" in the Greek language.

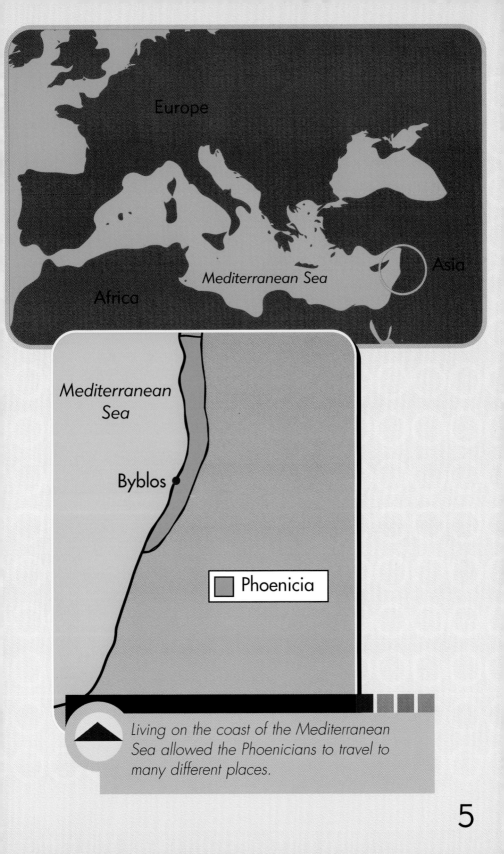

Europe

Mediterranean Sea

Africa

Asia

Mediterranean Sea

Byblos

Phoenicia

Living on the coast of the Mediterranean Sea allowed the Phoenicians to travel to many different places.

The ancient Phoenicians sold wood, cloth, metalwork, salt, and much more to people in other countries. The Phoenicians borrowed ideas and practices from these people. For example, they made some of their art similar to the art of people in Egypt.

Cuneiform was often written on statues and the walls of buildings.

Phoenicians also borrowed and used cuneiform, a kind of writing that was used in Mesopotamia since about 3000 B.C.

Phoenicians borrowed cuneiform from the Mesopotamians. Cuneiform was written by using a wedge-shaped stick to make characters in wet clay.

CREATING AN ALPHABET

The Phoenicians first used their own form of writing around 1400 B.C. They created an alphabet by changing the forms of earlier writing to create new forms. It is believed that the Phoenicians used Egyptian symbols when they made the signs for their new alphabet.

Egyptian symbols

Phoenician signs

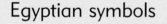

Byblos today

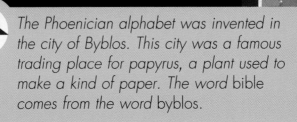

The Phoenician alphabet was invented in the city of Byblos. This city was a famous trading place for papyrus, a plant used to make a kind of paper. The word bible comes from the word byblos.

9

Phoenician writing used only 22 letters. Each letter stood for a sound used in the Phoenician language. There were no vowels used in their writing, only consonants. It is thought that the Phoenicians used their alphabet to write down things like business records and poetry.

Very few objects are left from the ancient Phoenicians. These are a few pieces of Phoenician art.

The Moabite Stone has Phoenician writing on it. King Mesha of Moab used it to tell about a war.

Clay tablets with Phoenician writing carved on them have been found. Phoenicians most likely used reeds or other sharp tools to write in the clay.

This sculpture is the oldest work from ancient Phoenicia to survive. It's from 1100 B.C.

Later, writing was done on papyrus. Papyrus, a tall water plant, could be pressed flat and made into paper.

Papyrus grows along the banks of some rivers near ancient Phoenicia.

FROM PHOENICIA TO THE WORLD

Phoenician writing was spread around the world as the Phoenicians traded with other countries.

CHECK IT OUT

▶ The word *alphabet* comes from the first two letters in the Greek alphabet, *alpha* and *beta*. These letters are very similar to the first two letters in the Phoenician alphabet, *aleph* and *beth*.

ALEPH

BETH

The Phoenician alphabet spread to parts of Africa, Asia, and Europe. The alphabet changed a little in each place it was used.

Phoenician boats could be rowed as well as sailed. This meant that Phoenicians could travel even when there was no wind.

The Phoenicians introduced the alphabet to the Greeks around 800 B.C. The Phoenicians also showed the Greeks the art of writing.

Phoenicians traveled hundreds of miles to trade their goods. Many of the records we have about the Phoenicians come from other countries.

17

The Greeks spread the alphabet to the Romans. Soon, it spread throughout many parts of Europe.

By the time the Phoenician alphabet made its way to Rome, it had been greatly changed.

	aleph	beth	gimel
Phoenician	∀	◁	⌐
	alpha	*beta*	*gamma*
Greek	∧	△	⟨
English	A	B	C

Many languages that are written today started with the Phoenician alphabet. The English, Spanish, Arabic, and Hebrew alphabets can all trace their beginnings back to the Phoenicians.

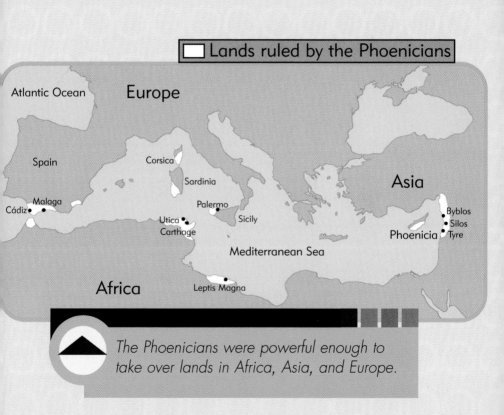

Lands ruled by the Phoenicians

Atlantic Ocean

Europe

Asia

Spain

Corsica

Sardinia

Palermo

Malaga

Cádiz

Utica

Carthage

Sicily

Byblos

Silos

Phoenicia Tyre

Mediterranean Sea

Africa

Leptis Magna

The Phoenicians were powerful enough to take over lands in Africa, Asia, and Europe.

19

THE GIFT OF THE PHOENICIANS

By 700 A.D., all of the areas where the Phoenicians once ruled were taken over by other countries. The Phoenician language slowly died out or became part of other languages. The most important thing the Phoenicians gave the world was their alphabet and way of writing.

Carthage was once a powerful Phoenician city. It was taken by the Romans in 146 B.C.

Glossary

consonants (**kahn**-suh-nuhnts) letters other than
  a, e, i, o, and *u*

cuneiform (kyoo-**nee**-uh-form) a form of writing that
  uses characters made up of simple wedge shapes

Mesopotamia (mehs-uh-puh-**tay**-mee-uh) an early
  civilization between the Tigris and Euphrates Rivers
  in present-day Iraq

papyrus (puh-**py**-ruhs) a tall water plant that is used
  to make a material much like paper

Phoenicia (foh-**nee**-shee-ah) an ancient civilization
  of traders and colonizers that lived around the
  Mediterranean Sea

reeds (**reedz**) tall grasses

sculpture (**skuhlp**-chuhr) a piece of art that has been
  made by cutting into stone, wood, or other things

symbols (**sihm**-buhlz) things that stand for something else

tablets (**tab**-lihts) blocks of clay that were used
  for writing

vowels (**vow**-uhlz) the letters *a, e, i, o,* and *u*

Resources

Books

Civilizations, Explorations, & Conquest
by Philip Wilkinson
Southwater Publishing (2001)

The Phoenicians
by Elsa Marston
Benchmark Books (2001)

Web Sites

Due to the changing nature of Internet links, PowerKids Press has developed an on-line list of Web sites related to the subjects of this book. This site is updated regularly. Please use this link to access the list:

http://www.powerkidslinks.com/waw/anph/

Index

Word Count: 450

Note to Librarians, Teachers, and Parents

If reading is a challenge, Reading Power is a solution! Reading Power is perfect for readers who want high-interest subject matter at an accessible reading level. These fact-filled, photo-illustrated books are designed for readers who want straightforward vocabulary, engaging topics, and a manageable reading experience. With clear picture/text correspondence, leveled Reading Power books put the reader in charge. Now readers have the power to get the information they want and the skills they need in a user-friendly format.